AGORAPHOBIA

A Recovered Victim's Perspective

About the Author

D.F. Nesto is a native Vermonter who lives in Connecticut with his wife, Mary Ann, a college librarian. He and his wife have five adult children and five grandchildren. He is:

1) A veteran, having served with the 82nd Air-borne Division;

2) A huge fan of both the Three Stooges and crossword puzzles; and

3) A licensed nursing home administrator, and holds a masters degree in Organizational Behavior.

D.F. Nesto has been involved with agoraphobia for nearly a quarter of a century.

AGORAPHOBIA

A Recovered Victim's Perspective

Help for Those Who Suffer From
Agoraphobia--From One Who
Has Had it and Found
His Way to Freedom.

Copyright © 2000 by D.F. Nesto
All rights reserved.

Soft-cover print versions published by
the Wellness Institute, Inc.
1007 Whitney Avenue, Gretna, LA 70056
August 1, 2000

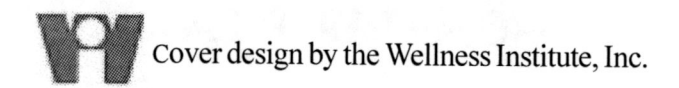

Cover design by the Wellness Institute, Inc.

SelfHelpBooks.com *is a division of the*

Wellness Institute, Inc.
Gretna, LA 70056

ISBN: 1-58741-042-7
Printed in the United States of America

Foreword

As a former paratrooper, I was required to jump out of an airplane from 1200 feet with a machine gun attached to my parachute harness. If the parachute fails, it takes eight seconds to hit the ground — four of which are spent in opening the parachute. As you can see, alertness is a mandatory requirement.

I am not suggesting that in order to recover, one must jump out of an airplane with a 30-cal machine gun attached. Quite the contrary.

I mention this only to make the point that seemingly courageous behavior such as that mentioned above does not exempt you from becoming a victim. Do not think that you are weak because you have agoraphobia.

Since I finished the book about one year ago, I have become a Grandfather for the fifth time, Paxil has been heavily advertised as an anti-anxiety medication, and based upon what I have been able to read, might be the drug of choice for a whole lot of anxieties.

When you read this book, you will know my position on the use of drugs as a weapon to fight agoraphobia. I prefer not to use medications, but far be it from me to even suggest that you stop taking whatever medications you are presently using. If they work for you, go for it! Personally, I prefer not to use drugs even though I did during the seven years that I was struggling. I found out, however, during the latter stages of my recovery, that I did not need them, nor did I want to use them.

As I sit here at my computer typing this page, I cannot help but reflect on the 18 years that have elapsed since I recovered, and wish that there were something else that I could do in order to show every victim that they too can recover.

After you read of my experiences and my struggle to recover, perhaps that will be enough to get you started on the road to recovery. I certainly hope so.

Good luck, and I wish you a speedy recovery.

DEDICATION

This book is dedicated to my wife, Mary Ann, whose thoughtful suggestions and keen editing ability made a somewhat technical book into something that is easily read and interesting.

Additionally, during the seven years that I was struggling to recover, she virtually had to raise our children, while maintaining her professional career as a Librarian.

Acknowledgments:

I would like to thank all of the people with whom I have worked, for sharing their experiences. Without their valuable input, this book would probably not have been written.

One last group that I would like to recognize are the countless thousands of victims who are still struggling to recover. Don't give up. You too can recover as I have. The key that will unlock the door that leads to recovery lies within yourself. Seek it like a devoted locksmith.

INTRODUCTION

The book that you are about to read is based upon my personal 24 year struggle with Agoraphobia: first, as an unsuspecting victim in 1974, then as a recovered Phobic seven years later, and finally through my association with a variety of support groups as a facilitator, from 1982 to 1996. During this nearly quarter of a century, I have had the opportunity to learn much about this misunderstood disorder as the result of my own recovery, as well as the struggles and pitfalls of the men and women with whom I have worked. The results of this experience have enabled me to view Agoraphobia from a variety of perspectives. My writing, therefore, is not only from my personal experience but also from the experience of the people with whom I have worked.

If you are an Agoraphobic:

Do you remember your first panic attack? Were you caught by surprise and ambushed? Do you remember every detail associated with that first attack — the time of day, the clothing you were wearing, why you were where you were when it happened? It is remarkably consistent among Agoraphobics, young and old, to remember every detail connected with that first attack, even if it happened 25 or more years ago.

Early Symptoms

What about those symptoms that came with that initial attack? Certainly you know the ones that I mean: the dizziness, blurred vision, hyperventilation, jelly-legs, chest pains and shortness of breath. Are those feelings of isolation and impending death still vivid in your mind? Can you recall thinking " **What if** . . .?" and then avoiding those places where the what if question arose? Of course you can.

If you can't, you are probably not an Agoraphobic.

Following a series of attacks, questions and avoidance, your next stop was at the doctor's office in order to find out what was happening to you. Did you learn anything? Probably not, since many physicians are not aware of Agoraphobia and so, consequently, are quick to prescribe medications in an effort to provide some relief from the terrifying symptoms. Valium, Xanax, and Tofranil are but a few of the medications that many, including myself, were given in an effort to ease the misery associated with this elusive, unknown affliction.

Recap

Let's recap the events. The first panic attack strikes without warning, then those terrifying symptoms descend on you like a suffocating blanket. Next there are more attacks in different places, visits to the doctor, medications, no definitive diagnosis. It is at this point that many victims report their world begins to get smaller and smaller as they avoid more and more. It is not uncommon for many victims to become prisoners in their own homes, fearful to leave because of the horrible symptoms. It is also a sad but true statement that many of these prisoners develop alcohol and drug addictions as the result of this imprisonment and the subsequent fear that *comes when attempting to leave.*

What this book can do for you.

Does any of this have a familiar ring to it? Have you had the physical symptoms checked out by a physician, eliminating them as having any medical consequence? If so, read on. This book can help you reclaim the self-confidence this affliction has stolen from you and get you started on the wonderful road to recovery. Please note: it is not my intent to set myself up as the world's greatest living expert on Agoraphobia, nor am I trying to belittle the efforts of those people who are working with victims. Rather, I am speaking from my base of experience. In this regard I feel a certain advantage because I have Agoraphobia, have overcome its stranglehold on my life, recovered from its devastating impact, and learned much about this misunderstood disorder in the process.

As I stated at the outset, I have

been an Agoraphobic for over 25 years and will continue to be, even though I have recovered. Don't be alarmed! Recovery means precisely that. There are no more symptoms, there are no more medications, there are no more "What ifs . . .?" avoidance, or deception. Recovery means that you will be able to do everything that the non-Phobic takes for granted. To deny the value of my experience in dealing with this affliction, out of some false sense of modesty, serves no useful purpose. I am writing of my success in order to help you recover. You can recover!

   I have used the words "he," or "him," for convenience sake. In no way should this usage be interpreted as a slight to women who are victims...

CHAPTER 1

WHAT IS AGORAPHOBIA?

What is Agoraphobia? Are you an Agoraphobic? How can you tell? Agoraphobia is not a mental illness; it is a disorder. Its symptoms trigger inappropriate fear reactions in a variety of situations that normally should not pose any threat to you.

Unfortunately, you don't know that and panic anyway. Think about it. There is no reason to become dizzy, hyperventilate, experience chest pain, or feel faint and weak when in a movie theater, restaurant, store, or driving on the highway. (Well, maybe driving on the highway, since this activity can make even the most serene and

Agoraphobia

peaceful person a physical wreck). At any rate, these seemingly harmless activities can and do create symptoms that victimize scores of people (estimates run as high as twenty million), who panic and flee from these and other situations.

Many Phobics report that their first attack came from out of the blue. Others report that their first attack resulted from a serious illness, the loss of a loved one, or some other traumatic event. Whatever the cause of the first attack and the attacks that follow, the victim is convinced that he is about to lose his mind or die, isolated and alone. It is fears such as these that keep the Phobic trapped and isolated, unable to perform the many activities of daily living that every non-phobic takes for granted. Take heart!

If you are truly Agoraphobic, the affliction is not life-threatening, although, when in the midst of a scorching panic attack, the victim could easily think that it was. Scared to death is not an issue.

Since many of the symptoms associated with Agoraphobia (dizziness, blurred vision, chest pain, hyperventilation, jelly-legs and weakness) could also be symptomatic of serious physical illness, such symptoms must be ruled out by a doctor as having any medical significance. As you know this process of elimination can be very expensive, time consuming, and vary from person to person. It is not uncommon for several years to elapse between the first panic attack, and a definitive diagnosis of Agoraphobia.

In my particular situation, it took seven years of pain, suffering, isolation and misery before I found out that what I was suffering had a name: **AGORAPHOBIA**

If this process of elimination is not enough to confuse and frustrate the victim, throw in other masquerades such as obsessive-compulsive disorder or hypoglycemia, and one can begin to understand why so much time elapses between onset of the symptoms and elimination of any physical cause.

The good news is the fact that after you have had the symptoms checked out, you can stop worrying about all those physical things that you might have felt trapped you for so long.

Now you can take control of your life and answer the questions posed at the beginning of this chapter.

What is Agoraphobia?

Agoraphobia is a series of physical symptoms that are inappropriate to the places and situations in which they occur. To the uninitiated victim, the symptoms are so frightening that he thinks the worse, e.g. fainting, heart attack, and death. It is not until any medical problems have been ruled out that progress can be made toward recovery. It would be virtually impossible to recover while still worrying about heart attacks, or death.

Ask Yourself

Am I an Agoraphobic? How can I tell? If you have any of the symptoms enumerated in the first paragraph, and they are not connected to some physical illness, welcome to the not-so-exclusive Agoraphobia club to which you, and millions of others, are active members.

Now that your fears about fainting, heart attack, death can be forgotten, go ahead and recover. You can, you know. What is there to be afraid of now except fear? The fears that have imprisoned you for so long don't matter anymore; you have just been paroled. Enjoy your newfound freedom.

D. F. Nesto

CHAPTER 2

STATISTICS AND VICTIMS

How many people suffer with this misunderstood demon? The answer to that question depends upon which statistics you choose to believe. I have read of numbers that vary between twenty million (20,000,000) and/or 10 % of the adult population. Whatever the accurate number is, it would have to include sufferers of panic attack, anxiety disorder, and Agoraphobia. I have not been able to determine whether or not these numbers include people struggling with these afflictions, unaware that it is Agoraphobia, so I am somewhat suspicious as to their validity.

From personal experience, I

struggled for seven long years, visited a variety of doctors, underwent a multitude of expensive tests (cardiograms, brain scans, blood studies, x-rays, etc.) before I found out that I had Agoraphobia . . . and then purely by accident. I also learned that Agoraphobia is not life threatening.

To the best of my knowledge, I have never heard of anyone dying as the result of a panic attack.

Agoraphobia: a man's or woman's disorder?

Another interesting twist to the question about the number of victims, is the gender of the victims. All too frequently I have read, and continue to read, about so-called "Experts" claiming that Agoraphobia is predominately a woman's disorder. I can tell you, unequivocally, that my experience shows there are an equal number of men and women with this disorder. I can also suggest to you that the reason for this misconception about the gender emphasis of this disorder is simple.

MEN ARE AFRAID TO ADMIT THE FACT THAT THEY HAVE AGORAPHOBIA.

Do you know why? Once again a simple answer. No self-respecting man would ever admit to a perception that is categorized as a **women's disorder.** Perhaps this has something to do with the male ego. Many men, including myself, initially go to unbelievable lengths to cover up the fact that they have this disorder.

As a victim attending group sessions and, later, as a facilitator of such sessions, I found out that there is no gender bias. Once I realized this, I stopped hiding and began to deal with my affliction openly. Unfortunately I cannot say the same for many of the male sufferers that I have known. The typical reaction is to live on the edge, shrouded in a cloak of fear, afraid to speak or seek help lest the "What if . . .?" syndrome kicks in.

- **"What if I tell someone?"**
- **"Will they think that I'm crazy?"**
- **"What about my masculinity?"**

Out of fear of exposure, men do not show up in the statistics as often as they should. Consequently, more incorrect gender assumptions are made, which leads to more men in hiding, and not getting the help that they so desperately need and want.

It is unfortunate that as long as there remains a gender bias, men are not likely to come out of hiding and admit to a disorder perceived as feminine. They will continue to hide, deny, and use whatever deceptive tactics they can in order to avoid discovery and reveal this weakness.

As the cover-up continues, men will continue to remain anonymous, and more incorrect conclusions will be drawn. Let me give you an example. I recently looked at a web site on the Internet that encourages people with the whole spectrum of panic, anxiety, and Agoraphobia, to write in and ask for help. Over a three-month period seventy percent (70%) of the respondents were women, and only thirty percent 30%) were men.

Unless my experience with this disorder is an anomaly, my guess is that there are probably somewhere between fifteen and twenty percent (15% - 20%) more men who would like to use this web site then those that actually did.

Agoraphobia

From one man to another, if you have any of the symptoms of Agoraphobia, do not hide or be ashamed to seek help.

Agoraphobia is no more a woman's disorder than bad teeth, acne, backache, or any other common malady.

As a matter of fact, Agoraphobia is an equal opportunity disorder since it does not discriminate on the basis of religion, sex, economics, or ethnicity. It strikes blacks, whites, Hispanics with equal force. It makes no difference if you are Catholic, Protestant, Jewish. Anyone can fall victim to this affliction.

Age does not exempt you. I have dealt with people, both male and female, as young as 18 and as old as 78.

Money does not buy you freedom from this misery; it cares not whether you are a millionaire or a pauper. It can strike anyone at any time and with equally devastating consequences.

As further support for my claim that there are probably as many men with Agoraphobia as women, read the following example.

I was involved with a support group, which was being taped by a local cable Television Station. There were eleven

people in the group, equally distributed between men and women. With the exception of myself, who was facilitating the group, not one man would consent to appear on camera.

This experience only serves to reinforce my contention that men do not show up in the statistics because they are much less likely to report the fact that they have Agoraphobia.

As a result, the statistics are drastically lopsided.

CHAPTER 3

ACCEPTANCE

Acceptance is a strategy that allows you to win by not fighting.

You have probably heard of the "fight-or-flight" reaction, which gives you the ability to do one or the other when confronted by danger and/or fear.

To the Phobic, doing either is the wrong thing. While it is true, initially, that all victims either fight or run from the symptoms, ask yourself the following question: Does either tactic work? More than likely, if it does, it will only be a temporary respite from the symptoms, with

Agoraphobia

no long-term benefit. You will not have the ability to go into the same fear-producing situation at a later date without again either fighting or running. There is an old adage that supports this position.

"He who fights and runs away, lives to fight or (run) another day."

What has been accomplished? Nothing but the opportunity to go into the fear-producing situation and lose again. This is a strategy that is counter-productive, time-consuming, and of no value in terms of recovery.

Running is just a temporary postponement of the inevitable arrival of the symptoms when the same situation or place must be faced again.

Is there any sensible reason to continue to run? To do so is to convince yourself that by running away you can eliminate the symptoms and make all of the fears disappear. Unfortunately the fears do disappear, but only for as long as you stay away from that place, or that situation.

If you allow yourself to be convinced that this behavior is a valid recovery strategy, you are setting yourself up for a restricted life style within a self imposed prison. Do not allow this to happen. Do not buy the idea that the worst will happen if you do not fight the symptoms, or run from them. This subtle trickery appears to work because when you flee, the symptoms go away, and if you fight, you merely prolong the point at which you run away. Can you see how this works to your disadvantage? The only thing that you accomplish by fighting or running is to guarantee the continuation of your imprisonment and inability to recover.

Have a doctor check your symptoms

I will say once again, go to your doctor and get all of your symptoms checked out, so that you can be assured that there is no medical reason for them. Once you do this you can proceed. If you have not done this, it is foolish, unwise, and dangerous to assume that they are related to Agoraphobia. Having done so, you can now move along to a discussion of acceptance in more detail.

What is acceptance?

Acceptance simply means that you can function in any situation with the presence of the symptoms and a panic attack. You now know that there is no physical basis for the symptoms, so you can unburdened yourself from the fear that you will faint, have a heart attack, or die.

None of these things will happen!

Example. Suppose you have somehow managed to go to church. You have already gone through your inventory of **"What ifs . . .?"**

You have found an end seat in the last row (just in case you have to make a speedy exit).

You begin to feel that old anxious feeling come over you. You steel yourself, ready to take whatever this evil demon can throw at you, suddenly it hits you with all of its power.

Your ears begin to burn, as the hair on the back of your neck feels as though it will ignite into a three-alarm fire. You begin to hyperventilate as your throat constricts, breathing becomes labored, and your chest begins to hurt. Your heart is beating so loudly that you think everyone in the church can hear it. (In reality no one else can).

"God, I am really having a heart attack this time! I must get out of

here. No, I must stay, my mind is trying to seduce me into believing that all of these feelings are life threatening. Should I fight? No that is the wrong thing to do. I must get out of here right now!"

So out the door you go like an Olympic sprinter.

A quick recap of the process that has just occurred will show you just how powerful acceptance can be in helping you on to the road to recovery.

Whether you realize it or not, acceptance has been involved from start to finish in this little drama. When you made your hasty exit from the church after a valiant, but fruitless, effort to stay, you accepted the fact that when you were in church, you would not be okay. Sure enough you were not okay.

You also accepted the fact that once you fled to the outside, you would be okay. Sure enough once again, you were okay.

You have scored another victory over yourself, and **lost a golden opportunity to take a step, however tentative, in the direction of recovery.** In behavioral terms, your behavior

Agoraphobia

(fighting and then running) was rewarded since the symptoms disappeared.

Acceptance worked in both situations. In fact, you were involved in the very act that would enable you to begin the recovery process, but for all of the wrong reasons. You pulled the trigger that fired the way you felt and acted. Acceptance in this case was merely the bullet that sped you out the door.

This acceptance is powerful stuff, if you use it to your advantage. Unfortunately in this case you did as many others, including myself, have done in similar circumstances. You fought the symptoms and then fled when they became unbearable.

They were unbearable because you did not accept them as being of no medical consequence.

Positive outcomes

Please think about this. Acceptance worked because you accepted certain negative outcomes and your acceptance made them happen. The same process can work to produce a positive outcome if you would only give it a chance. It is completely up to you.

Having said all of this, try this

the next time you are in a fear-producing place or situation. **Do not fight or flee. Accept the fact that nothing bad will happen to you as the result of having the symptoms. Stay in the place or situation as long as you can without fighting. When you cannot stay any longer, do not flee like a scared rabbit. Give yourself permission to leave, then get up calmly and leave.**

On the surface this may seem like fighting and fleeing once again. It is neither. What happens is a very significant event. You will have taken control of the situation instead of the symptoms or the fear controlling you. You may leave because you have given yourself permission to do so.

The symptoms will not have driven you from the place. A very subtle transfer of control from the fear to you will have occurred. When you do this, you will have accomplished a significant victory. This becomes a foundation on which you can build. Use it in other places and situations; it will serve you well.

CHAPTER 4

THE "WHAT IF...?" SYNDROME

The Agoraphobic is a master at imagining negative outcomes. It makes no difference what the situation or the place; he will raise the **"What if . . .?"** question and come up with a variety of answers (a.k.a. excuses) that will guarantee his absence from that place or situation. **"What if...I go to a restaurant and get sick?" "What if...** I get those funny feelings?" **"What if . . .** I can't get a seat by the door?"

Questions such as these, or any others that you might be able to think

Agoraphobia

of, will guarantee that you will never be caught by surprise. Thus protected, the risk of making a fool of yourself or worse, if you have to make a hasty departure from the situation, is virtually eliminated. The result of this behavior means that you will not go into this, or any other fear-producing situation or place, thereby denying yourself the opportunity to cope (in the right way—remember **Chapter 3: Acceptance)** and derive some benefit from it. A good point to remember: **Recovery lies in the places and situations you fear most.**

Agoraphobic behavior

Once again you have retreated. Once again you have not taken advantage of an opportunity in which huge benefits could have accrued to you, and sadly, one more negative outcome and self-doubt.

As an Agoraphobic, is this behavior recognizable? Can you deny the fact that you have done the same thing in similar situations? I am sure you can. However is it true, or just self-deception, and more self-protection?

Let's take an example. Suppose that you have been asked to go to a movie.

Would you tell the person who asked you that you have Agoraphobia, and that you are afraid that you will have a panic attack if you go? More than likely you will say, "I don't like the actor," "It's too expensive," " . . . too far," "I don't feel like going." Anything but the truth. The person who asked you is none the wiser, and once again you have pulled off another deceptive act to your disadvantage. Another point to ponder:

**Keep a fear private—
it will control your behavior.**

**Make a fear public—
it will lose its power to control.**

The effect of "What if . . .?"
The seductive nature of the **"What if . . .?"** syndrome is its ability to lure you into a false sense of security by preventing you from going into situations that produce the dreaded symptoms. When you can't drive your car on the highway nor do many of the other routine things that others take for granted, you more than likely have **"What if'd . . .?"** yourself into an avoidance of those situations.

In so doing, the avoidance has proven the **"What if . . .?"** to be correct.

"What if... I get a panic attack while driving on the highway?" **"What if...** I have to abandon my car and go screaming off into God knows where?"

"What if . . . I cause an accident involving innocent people?"

Because of the answers you give yourself to the **"What if . . .?"** questions, you don't have to face the fear, you don't have to endure the symptoms, and you don't have to recover.

It is entirely up to you. These kinds of assumptions terrify you and cause you to stop (avoid) driving, out of fear that these seductive assumptions will make your worse fears a reality. Consequently because of the assumption, the avoidance makes the symptoms disappear.

Seduction wins again, and you lose again. Don't fall for it, face it (accept it) and move forward.

The entire process of **"What if . . .?"** and its seductive cousin, avoidance, while appearing to work, does not. The only thing that works in this situation is your assumptions, and they are working against you.

Remember:

Recovery lies in the places and situations that you fear the most. Seek them as you would a coveted reward.

Productive strategies

There are more productive strategies that you can use in your path to recovery. For example: try saying: "So **what if** . . .?" All you need to do is believe in your own ability to succeed. Instead of "**What if?**" and avoid, try " **So what if . . .?**" **and then do.**

It is the fear of the symptoms and the assumptions that go with them that imprison you, not the places and situations.

Think about it. Are there any reasons to fear going to a restaurant, or leaving your home, or going to a movie? Of course there aren't.

The cause of the problems is the feelings that develop in those places and situations, the ultimate being a fear that those feelings will escalate into a full blown panic attack from which there is no (perceived) escape. The fear of either going insane or dying, is perhaps the most compelling. Either one cause the most anxiety and urgent need for avoidance in order to stop them from occurring.

The absolute importance of a medical check-up

As I mentioned earlier, one must believe that nothing of medical significance will happen. In order to believe this to be the case, all physical symptoms must be checked out in order to eliminate any and all physical basis. Once this has been done you need not worry about insanity, or death, heart attack, fainting, or any of the other disasters, which you just know are waiting to happen. Don't worry because these things won't happen. You just think (accept) that they will, which is enough to prevent you from doing just about anything.

Taking responsibility

I fully realize that my telling you these things will not automatically make them happen. You have to take some responsibility for your own behavior and help yourself. I can only tell you what works. You must apply the things I offer in order to make it work for you. First, you must accept the fact that nothing bad will happen to you. When I use the word accept, it must be a willing acceptance. Lip service accomplishes nothing; you must be willing. Failure to accept the situation as being non-threatening will result in fighting the symptoms, which in turn will guarantee a failure to recover.

I cannot overemphasize the value of acceptance, since it is the basis upon which recovery will occur.

There is no such thing as failure if there is a willing acceptance of taking the risk involved in recovery.
Failure can only occur if you don't try.

CHAPTER 5

THE GREAT PUZZLE!

One of the puzzling aspects about Agoraphobia is its ability to masquerade as other things. Phobias can masquerade as medical problems, and vice versa.

Many of the symptoms associated with Agoraphobia, such as dizziness, blurred vision, pain in the chest, tremors, can also be the symptoms of medical problems. Hypoglycemia, a depletion of blood sugar, can also produce many of the symptoms of Agoraphobia.

In addition to these masquerades, a further complication that interferes with an accurate diagnosis is the ability of the victim to deceive others regarding the reasons he is reluctant to go to a restaurant, a movie, leave home, or do any of the routine activities that non-victims take for granted.

For all of these reasons you must visit your doctor and have the symptoms checked out, thus eliminating them as having any medical significance.

Let me give you another example that reinforces the puzzling nature of this disorder. I was facilitating a support group in which a young woman was a member. She explained that she was experiencing many of the classic symptoms of Agoraphobia as the result of an automobile accident in which her lung collapsed While there was no medical reason for her to fear a recurrence of a collapsed lung, she began to develop anxiety along with panic attacks. Because of this, she began to avoid doing many activities that she had previously done effortlessly.

Another interesting question that enters into this enigma is the connection between Agoraphobia and depression.

Similar to the question about which came first, the chicken or the egg, so it is with Agoraphobia and depression. Does Agoraphobia cause depression, or vice versa?

Once again I can speak from my own experience, and that experience shouts:

***"I became depressed after
I developed Agoraphobia."***

In support of this position, let's look at the facts in my own situation. First, I was beset by a myriad of frightening symptoms, suffered an existence that became more hermit-like with each passing day, found myself imprisoned in my home, developed a shattered self-image, experienced a total loss of confidence regarding everything, and, finally, withdrew from practically everything. Add this to my misery index and the ever-present fear that lurked and surrounded me like a cloak and perhaps you will understand when I say, **"Who wouldn't get depressed?"**

I remain unconvinced that depression causes Agoraphobia. The title of this chapter, **"The Great Puzzle!"** aptly describes the search undertaken by every victim in an effort to explain the array of frightening symptoms. The constant visits to the doctor with

Agoraphobia

endless and expensive medical tests that continually come back negative are a large part of the puzzle. Brain scans, blood studies, x rays, cardiograms, GI series, chest studies, in short, every conceivable test, is done so that any medical basis for the symptoms can be eliminated. Amidst this blizzard of tests and analysis, the cash register continues to ring up more and more expensive medical costs. The results continue to be negative and you remain in the dark.

Does this process strike a familiar note? Can there be any doubt why you feel alone and frustrated, as the reasons for the terrifying symptoms remain unnamed? Having said all of this maybe you can understand why I am skeptical about the claims that depression causes Agoraphobia. Quite the opposite is often true.

D. F. Nesto

CHAPTER 6

EFFECTIVE TREATMENTS

As you can see there are many puzzling aspects to this scary affliction and an equal number of so-called effective treatments. As I struggled for seven long years trying to recover, there were a multitude of alleged treatments around, but I was not able to find any that could enable me to get into a car for a trip on the highway, be comfortable in a restaurant, go to a shopping mall, a grocery store or a theater.

I have listed a few of the strategies that are supposed to work. Do you recognize any of them?

- Thought switching
- Drug therapy
- Bio Feedback
- Inflicting pain via the use of a rubber band around your wrist

These are but a few of the techniques that are supposed to help. I am unable to endorse any of them since I tried them all and found them to be useless. While they did not work for me, they may work for you. Let me give you an example. It is absolutely impossible for me to understand how, when in the midst of a scorching panic attack, anyone can switch thoughts and have the presence of mind to say, "Wait! I am having a panic attack and I am terrified that something terrible is going to happen to me, death being the worst, closely followed by heart attack, fainting, or bizarre behavior."

Given the negative thoughts that occur during a panic attack, this Thought Switching technique advises you to switch your thoughts to a sandy beach and a beautiful blue ocean, where the panic attack will be washed away on the crest of a softly breaking wave. If you believe that, I have a bridge in Brooklyn that I would love to sell to you.

Seriously, anyone silly enough to believe thought switching is possible has never had a full-blown panic attack and never felt the back of his neck ignite like dry leaves under the flame of an Ohio Blue Tip Match.

Another treatment that is used extensively is Drug Therapy. It is frightening to me to see the number of people who have been diagnosed with Agoraphobia and are taking prescription drugs in order to combat the symptoms. Xanax, Valium, Tofranil, to name but a few. Once again, in desperation, I too took the drugs mentioned above, as well as others, and was seriously concerned about addiction.

This concern was reinforced by the fact that the prescribed medications did not make the entrance to any fear-producing situation easier, or possible. As you can see, I am not a big supporter of drugs as a means of recovery from Agoraphobia. They didn't work for me. If you have tried, or want to try, them and they work for you, more power to you

I want to emphasize in the strongest possible terms, do not decide to stop taking any medications that a

physician has prescribed, unless that same physician allows you to do so under his supervision.

My position is based on my own experience and with the strategies that I employed in my own recovery.

As such, I prefer not to use any of the medications presently being used to treat Agoraphobia, since I have not found them effective.

What then is left to you, the victim, suffering alone, scared, confused, helpless, and hopeless, after the quick fixes have been exhausted?

What can you do to cope with these yet-to-be-identified symptoms? Unfortunately, the agonizing process of elimination must begin. More than likely you have gone through this process yourself. Doctor, after doctor, expense after expense, in search of answers that remain elusive. As each new test comes back negative, a sense of despair and depression sets in, driving many to medications as a last resort. I know, from personal experience, that several people I met along the way to recovery began drinking in order to cope with their symptoms.

It is not uncommon to encounter victims of Agoraphobia who are addicted to both alcohol and drugs.

Obviously, these people now have three problems: Agoraphobia, alcoholism, and drug addiction. Given the abundance of misunderstanding that surrounds this disorder, it doesn't surprise me that there are so many unrecovered Agoraphobics.

It is tragic that for many the struggle will go on in a hopeless kind of way, as they continuously seek answers to the question about what it is that is tormenting them. I see this eternal search as a kind of treadmill upon which untold numbers of people follow a predetermined cycle of despair and disappointment. The cycle consists of scary symptoms, identification attempts, doctor after doctor, test after test, failed recovery attempts, empty treatment promises, drugs, alcohol, and deepening depression.

There is hope!

Amidst this entire gloomy outlook, however, there is hope.

You can recover and begin to lead a normal life once again. There is a right way to recover and in my opinion, it does not involve the use of drugs. The point in writing this book is to show you, if you are an Agoraphobic, how to recover, get off the treadmill, and accelerate the entire process from initial onset to freedom and normalcy. I am confident that, as this happens, there will be fewer on the treadmill and more on the path to recovery. This can only happen when the mystery is taken out of this disorder by speeding up the process of identification and recovery, bringing a stop to the endless amount of suffering.

Helping hands

As more and more of us find our way to recovery, we in turn can help others as we have been helped. I believe in the old adage: **"Experience is the best teacher."** Nothing could be more accurate than the application of this adage in the treatment and recovery from Agoraphobia. There is ample evidence supporting this position. Recovered alcoholics and drug addicts head up many of the most successful drug and alcohol treatment programs. The same can be true with Agoraphobia.

The recovered Agoraphobic knows all the tricks and deceptions. There is a complete understanding of the " **What if . . .?"** and **"Avoidance"** syndromes,

Agoraphobia

as well as other counterfeit behaviors employed by Agoraphobics. The recovered person has been through the panic attacks, the medications, and the quick fixes.

In short, he has been through it all, and has probably discovered that one of the best and safest ways to recover is via the natural process of **Acceptance.**

As simple as this might sound, it absolutely works. When applied to the treatment of Agoraphobia, it takes on the power of a dynamo.

Once you have learned to accept the fact that your symptoms are of no medical consequence **(you have checked them out with a doctor, right?)** and found out that:

1. they have a name,
2. they are not fatal, and
3. they will not make you behave in a bizarre manner,

You can then begin the serious and rewarding business of recovery.

The Confidence Bank

In order to recover, you must work with someone who has recovered and regained his confidence. This person can **"Loan"** you as much confidence as you need in order to aid you in your recovery.

When you no longer need to **"Borrow"** confidence, you are well on your way to recovery, and then you can become a **"Confidence bank"** and make a **"Confidence loan"** to someone else.

As this begins to happen, the treadmill process has to slow down and/or stop. As a result the identification process will become much faster, and much less expensive. Much the same as the "Rock in the pond," the recovery ripples will extend far beyond that recovered person.

CHAPTER 7

ACCEPTANCE, DECEPTION, AVOIDANCE

Three of the most critical aspects involved in your recovery from Agoraphobia are:

1. acceptance,
2. deception, and
3. avoidance.

The latter two, deception and avoidance, are the seductive pair that keep you frightened as they bombard you with their arsenal of terror.

Acceptance is in a constant struggle

Agoraphobia

with these two demons in their attempt to convince you that they cannot harm you if you just accept their powerlessness as fact. You need not be a rocket scientist to realize that the deck is stacked in favor of the two demons because of their past success.

They derive their power from their past success, aided by your fear of someone "finding out" that you have a problem. When taken together, you have no other logical choice but to conclude that avoidance of any fear-producing situation is a sure-fire way to avoid the scary symptoms.

It is the fear of the symptoms that make avoidance and deception so seductively easy

For example: that first scorching panic attack you experienced is etched in your mind so strongly that you can remember it as easily as you do your own name. While you are still searching for answers, anything that will ease the pain connected with the symptoms you are experiencing, you will embrace like a long lost lover.

A simple invitation to go for a walk will immediately activate your mental computer, which will gladly generate a whole host of **"What ifs . . .?"**

These seemingly valid reasons are as real to you as the fear that you know will overtake you if you answer, "Yes" to the invitation.

> **"What if I have an attack while walking?"**
>
> **"How can I hide it?"**
>
> **"What can I say is happening if I start to shake?"**
>
> **"What excuse can I fabricate so that I can turn around and return to a place where I feel secure?"**

Just thinking about the answers to these **"What ifs . . .?"** makes you shiver with fear. Can you give any reasons to conceal the fear and say **"No thank you"** to the invitation?

> **"I'm not feeling well today, maybe another time"**
>
> **"I have a lot of things to do, checks to write, calls to make."**

Any time a routine task is being considered, a whole host of **"What ifs . . .?"** will negate the possibility of your even trying. As long as you allow this behavior to continue **(Avoidance and Deception)** you will remain a victim, and each and every opportunity that arises will be declined with perfectly legitimate sounding reasons (Excuses).

Deception will, once again, win, and you have, once again, missed an opportunity to make some progress. Once again the evil pair has seized control and pushed **Acceptance** into the background while reinforcing the idea that **Avoidance and Deception** are effective coping strategies. Doesn't this kind of cowardice make you furious enough to want to do something about it?

You must resist this clever trap with all the strength and courage that you can muster. To do otherwise is to strengthen the power and control that you have already given to these two demons so that they can continue to use it, even more effectively, against you and continue to make a mess of your life. Do you really want this to happen? Think about it!

While this act of cowardice (**Avoidance and Deception**) is going on, you allow the shift in control to eliminate the opportunity to use **Acceptance** as a recovery tool.

Because you allow **Avoidance and Deception** to control, you allowed this lost opportunity to happen. In the process, you were convinced that these two "shams" were effective strategies. You must also accept the fact that you will never be free or have any chance at recovery unless you reject these demons. Show them up for what they really are - seductive, evil thieves.

You must be willing

I seriously doubt that you want to be a prisoner, because I know from experience that every victim that I have met along the way yearns to be free and to be able to do all of the routine things that everyone else takes for granted. You can!

You must be willing to take those first steps toward Acceptance and venture out into the sunlight of freedom.

I am not unaware of the pain and difficulty involved in staring fear in the face and willingly accepting it as nothing more than your mind playing games with you. It is not easy, but it is worth it.

I fully realize how difficult it is to accept all of those scary feelings. Even though you know that they are of no medical significance, they are still scary enough to make you want to avoid them. How then can you overcome the odds and go on to recovery?

Is there no hope? There doesn't seem to be any reward for enduring that horrible experience. How can you resist and accept when every fiber in your body is screaming at you, telling you to run away? How many times will you have to go through this terror before it loses its power over you?

No resistance

The answer to these questions is really quite simple: **Acceptance!** It will take as long as it takes. You win by not resisting. Once you have mastered the skill of taking the fear out of fear, then, and only then, will the terror loose its power over you.

Perhaps the best way to illustrate the point is to give you an example. If I could give you an iron clad guarantee that by doing the things that I have suggested, you would recover, you certainly would do them, right? Of course you would. Why not go for it?

Give yourself permission

Think about this. I read somewhere that the average panic attack lasts about 30-45 seconds (although when in the middle of one it seems like a lifetime). I can only encourage you to continue trying, taking strength in the knowledge that you will not faint, you will not have a heart attack, nor will you die. The one thing about which you can be certain is the fact that you will make a speedy exit from the situation.

The bottom line for you is to willingly go into the fear producing situation, stay as long as you can, without resisting, and when you cannot stay any longer, give yourself permission to leave.

At this point, get up quietly and leave. In so doing you have seized control of the situation, wresting it

Agoraphobia

from the two demons of despair and control. The club of fear, which this duo has been holding over your head with the threat of it dropping, will have been removed. The benefit to you, derived from your seizing control by facing the fear the right way, will be the boost in your confidence level. This boost of confidence serves as a springboard that will propel you into becoming more courageous, and attempting to (willingly) try to do more and more.

A willingness to try
Don't be discouraged if the same things that scared you before begin to happen following your first success. Do the same thing again as you did the first time and success will again be yours.
Remember, a willingness to try and not succeed is not a failure.
Failure can only occur when you allow the twin demons to force you to flee from a situation out of fear of the symptoms.

A different type of war
You may wonder why I use such terms as enemy, control, etc. In much the same way as an enemy wages war, so it

is with Agoraphobia. You are literally at war with an enemy whose objective is the total domination of your life. At first glance, it would seem as though the enemy has everything in its arsenal that is needed to dominate your life. However, by looking closer you will be able to see the difference between your private war and the conventional war.

Your private war will be won by not fighting. You are victorious by accepting. There have been several famous leaders who achieved their ends by passive resistance, in much the same way that I am suggesting to you.

From that first scorching panic attack until you willingly accept the next one, recovery will be delayed and a carefree life denied. I know that you are fearful simply reading about what you have to do in order to recover. Please trust me; I know the feeling. I was as fearful as you are now when I first decided to willingly face that next panic attack, and actually invite it to hit me with its best shot.

It will be a rewarding feeling when you realize that you are doing what you previously went to great lengths to avoid.

Agoraphobia

I remember the first time I prepared to do this and recall how the mere thought of doing it sent icy shivers of fear through out my body. When I did it, and won, the shivers were replaced by a warm glow of victory.

This is an excellent example of being able to ignore the false messages your mind is sending you. You have to do what you have to do if you are to recover. This means walking into any fear-producing situation, and willingly facing the fear head on, taking whatever it has to throw at you and throwing it right back. Having done this you will experience the feeling of wholeness and control.

D. F. Nesto

CHAPTER 8

FEAR OF EXPOSURE

One of the most closely guarded secrets that is shared by most of us Agoraphobics, is that we have this disorder. We act as though we are being punished for committing some heinous crime and we must not reveal it to anyone. We go to extreme lengths in an effort to keep this shame from nearly everyone. The process involves intricate patterns of lies and deception that are, on the surface, both plausible and reasonable to the untrained, but not to the fellow sufferer.

Why is this true? There is a simple answer to that question. The fellow sufferer has probably used many of the of the same excuses, and quickly recognizes them for exactly what they are.

The basis for this feeling of inadequacy is probably connected to the fact that this disorder has stolen our self-image and confidence, leaving us with the idea that we are less of a person, and therefore deserve the punishment.

Stop punishing yourself

If you feel this way, give yourself a break. You don't deserve this affliction any more or less than the man next door, the women in the store, or anyone else for that matter. What happens, happens. If you don't get one thing, you get another. Stop punishing yourself, you have enough of a load to carry. Don't make the load any heavier than it already is.

Do not feel as though you are the only one that feels this way. During my recovery, and afterwards as well, I met many sufferers who felt this way, and they too were inflicting unnecessary shame and punishment on themselves.

Don't do it. To do so adds one more obstacle that must be removed before you can recover. I can fully understand why you might feel this way. I felt the same way myself when I was struggling to recover. Do yourself a favor. Lose that feeling!

Making a fear public

You also need to give up the fear of being "found out" and begin telling everyone that you have Agoraphobia. Use everyone in any way possible in order to do that.

> **When you keep a fear secret, it controls your behavior.**
>
> **When you make a fear public, it loses its power to control your behavior.**

These are words that you can take to the bank. Do not deceive. Do not avoid. Tell everyone that you are an Agoraphobic. The truth will set you free.

Making a fear public strips the fear of its power to control, thus enabling you to give up the fear. You will be absolutely amazed at the great weight that will be lifted off your shoulders when you tell everyone that you have Agoraphobia. When you do this you no longer have to lie about why you can't do certain things (and all the while you are suffering silently because you can't).

An example:

Try this example, as reinforcement of this idea, and you will see why the weight will seem lighter. Let's assume that you are in a supermarket. As you begin to fill your wagon with a variety of groceries, the dreaded feelings that you were afraid would come when you forced yourself to enter, arrive with a BANG.

Instead of running out of the store like a scared rabbit, find someone in the store that looks non-threatening, approach that person and explain what is happening to you and why. More than likely he will not understand what Agoraphobia is, but will understand what a panic attack is all about. Don't be afraid, just do it.

What harm can come of it? Embarrassment, and shame? Neither of those things will happen. The person will not harm you nor ridicule you, or do

Agoraphobia

any of the things that you imagined.

Au contraire—that person will be sympathetic since most people are willing to be helpful. More important than being able to give up your fear of approaching a stranger and asking for help, will be the fact that you did and it worked. You will notice that by "'fessing up", the fear was made public and it lost its power to control. You have just unlearned a learned fear. The next time that you have a need to "use" someone, it will be much easier. Practice makes perfect.

Incidentally the person who you approach will feel good about himself or herself because they helped someone. Everybody is a winner.

D. F. Nesto

CHAPTER 9

THE SUBTLE FIGHT

I have stressed the importance of accepting fear as the most effective method in your struggle to recover. One of the main obstacles that stands in the way of accepting fear is our natural inclination to fight.

> **Fighting is the worst tactic that you can use in your struggle to recover.**

I understand that fighting is a natural defense against anything that is legitimately frightening. However, to do so in this case is to virtually guarantee failure. When our defenses go up, physiological changes begin to occur. We get a rush of adrenaline which enables us to fight or run. While this fight or run capability is a valuable asset when confronted by a real danger, it serves only as fuel for a panic attack when the fear is inappropriate.

Working around the apparent enigma

Given this apparent enigma, what can you do when confronted by a situation that oozes ominous messages about fainting or dying? As I have stated before, nothing bad is going to happen to you. It is precisely those fears, and your reaction to them, that keep an obstacle between you and recovery.

You have to jump over that obstacle and willingly accept the heat and ride out the storm. When you allow yourself to be seduced into behavior that is counterfeit, you become your own worse enemy. This is the subtle fight that I referred to at the beginning of the chapter.

Let me give you another example. Let us assume that you have somehow managed to get yourself to church unescorted. There you sit (probably in the last row closest to the door,

Agoraphobia

just in case) tense, nervous. Your mind begins to work on your memory, recalling problems that you have experienced in church in the past. This time you are really determined to make it. Unbeknownst to you, the seeds of failure have already been planted by virtue of your grim determination.

"I'll I make it this time, or else."

There you sit, poised and ready, as you wait for the inevitable enemy to strike. Silently you speak to God.

"Why are you making me feel this way?"
"Help me. I am in your house."

Does this sound like acceptance, or is it just one more cleverly concealed escape that you have designed in order not to accept? Ask yourself the following question: "Isn't it true that I knew I was not willingly ready to face and accept the fear the right way?" I would be willing to bet that when you forced yourself to go, you arrived primed and ready to panic. Upon entering the church, you probably thanked God for the empty seat in the last row, just in case you had to make a speedy departure without drawing a lot of attention to your flight.

Expected outcomes and why they occur

Guess what? The symptoms arrived on cue, you undoubtedly gritted your teeth and hung onto the pew with a death grip, then fled like a scared rabbit. Once you were outside, the symptoms vanished, right? You felt better getting out, and in so doing you reinforced the old idea that fleeing is an effective strategy.

In one way, it really is. It is effective insofar as seducing you, once again, into believing just the opposite of the right way to recover.

Let's talk about what really happened. Without realizing it you have been engaged in a subtle fight, no less vigorous than would be the case if you were in a street fight. As another part of this subtle fight, you also accepted (subtly) the following outcome.

"When I am in church I won't feel right, I will get those funny feelings again, scared, uncomfortable, edgy, off balance, dizzy".

Sure enough, all of those things happened. When the pressure reached the point where you were convinced that your head would begin to smoke, out the door you went, thankful to be out before you fainted or worse. Once outside a miraculous event occurred, one that you wished had occurred inside.

Your symptoms disappeared, you felt better, you were relieved, and the fire went out. Another subtle fight has just been completed, and once again you were the loser.

Your acceptance of the outcome

Just as surely as you are reading these lines, you accepted a negative outcome while in church and a positive outcome once outside. Can you see how seductively subtle your fighting behavior was?

"Inside I am going to get symptoms, outside I will feel better."

Both situations turned out just the way you allowed them to turn out, but for all of the wrong reasons. If only you were able to willingly do the things in church and out of church, that you involuntarily did, you would not have had to flee, in the first place. Sounds kind of convoluted, but it's accurate, nonetheless.

In the example above, one additional subtlety has taken place. The **Avoidance** syndrome has once again reared its ugly head.

"If I avoid (run from) those places that create the bad feelings, I won't get the feelings." You have been subtly seduced into believing that the symptoms will only come when you go into places that you fear. In reality the exact opposite occurs. The symptoms come because you allow them to come in those places which you fear. Conversely the symptoms will not come in those places that you don't fear—outside in this case. In both situations the key, or lack thereof, is acceptance of the outcome.

This chapter has focused on the subtleties involved in fighting. Before you can do anything about ending the subtle fight, you must be aware that you are doing it. Once you become aware that you are doing it, you can practice not doing it, and take another step toward recovery.

Remember the following

"You are unaware that you are unaware...becoming aware that you are unaware is a huge step."

One additional piece of information to think about is the following.
Doesn't it make sense to go through a panic attack in the right way and derive some benefit from it that you

can use in similar, or different, situations?

The right way is to recognize, and accept, that you won't do any of the things or experience any of the feelings that have kept you a prisoner. In the words of Franklin Roosevelt,

"We have nothing to fear but fear itself."

D. F. Nesto

CHAPTER 10

TRUISMS

Everything in our society has truths and myths, and so it is with Agoraphobia. I have enumerated a few of the truths that I discovered along the way to recovery. Perhaps when you read them, you will find them helpful and comforting.

1. Recovery Lies In the Places You Fear.
2. Make A Fear Public—It Will Lose Its Power To Control.
3. Keep A Fear Private—It Will Control Your Behavior.

4. The Pocket Clutch.
5. The Bully Syndrome.
6. The Trusted Companion.
7. The Safety Zone.
8. The Confidence Account.
9. Benefits of Agoraphobia.

The Last Fear Before Recovery -- Let's look at each of the above.

1. RECOVERY LIES IN THE PLACES YOU FEAR

This is a valuable asset in the recovery process. It requires you to confront the fears by willingly entering those places and doing those things that you have been avoiding for so long. It is understandable why you might be apprehensive about this suggestion, however, you must be able to ignore the false messages that your memory has been sending you. Look at it this way. If I could guarantee your recovery by doing this, you most certainly would do it, right? Of course you would. I can do better than that. I can give you an ironclad promise that if you do these things you will recover. I know, because I did them myself, and I recovered.

Now go ahead and do them, it is okay to be afraid, but don't let the

Agoraphobia

fear stand in your way.

If you are not successful the first or second or third time, etc. that you try, do not punish yourself, and think that you are a failure. It does not matter. You did not develop Agoraphobia overnight, nor will you recover overnight. It takes as long as it takes. Don't forget the fact that you have been a helpful partner, however unwilling, in the development of this disorder.

There is no timetable for recovery. Don't get impatient. Recovery varies from person to person, and is contingent upon how courageous you are willing to be. The important thing to remember is that nothing bad is going to happen to you when you confront your fears. You are not going to faint, or die, or have any of the other things that you fear, happen.

As you begin to take these courageous steps toward recovery, remember that you must face them willingly.

Accept the fears and float through them. I can tell you from experience that when you do this you will feel a calm confidence that you have not felt in years. Now go for it!

2. **Make A Fear Public—
   It Will Lose Its Power To Control;
   and:**

3. **Keep A Fear Private—
   It Will Control Your Behavior.**

If there is a more beneficial recovery strategy then this one, I have not found it in all my years of experience with Agoraphobia.

Let's analyze this strategy. When you buy the false messages that your memory is sending you, you give them strength while weakening your own confidence. This response will reinforce the false notion that you are sick and using deception, denial, and concealment is the only way to prevent that from becoming known to others. Your fear of being "found out" will lead to feelings of rejection, unworthiness, and belief that you are deserving of scorn. You certainly don't want that to happen. What do you do? You conceal, deceive, and deny. These kinds of responses are destructive, and counter-productive, and succeed only in preventing you from achieving your coveted goal of recovery. Instead of concealment and denial, substitute a

Agoraphobia

willingness to reveal, to be open and up front. Once you have done this, it will feel as though a giant weight has been lifted off your shoulders.

Admitting to the fact that you have Agoraphobia is not some dreadful sin to be ashamed of. You have done nothing wrong. You are still the same person that you have always been, although buried under a pile of fear. Get your recovery shovel and dig yourself out. The time is right. Tell everyone. Open up, don't be ashamed

4. THE POCKET CLUTCH:

This is one of my favorites because when I discovered its hold on me, I became free, once and for all. It also showed me just how powerful this disorder could be, even after you think you have recovered.

Most of us, at one time or another, have visited a doctor in our search for answers.

As a result we were given one of the many anti-anxiety drugs in an effort to ease the symptoms. I have already mentioned my position on drugs, so I won't mention it again. At any rate we have all used them, with variable results. After struggling to give up the medication **(Again, do not go** off a medication unless it is done under the supervision of the doctor that originally prescribed it), I finally began doing the things that in the past I had found to be impossible.

Such things as driving a car on the highway, going to a McDonald's by myself, seeing a movie with a friend, all done without the excuses. In short, I was doing all of the things that everyone else was doing.

Things looked fine and, after seven long, painful years, I was recovered, or so I thought—until this demon, suddenly, and unexpectedly, threw another shot at me. One morning, as I was getting ready to go to work (you can have a job and Agoraphobia at the same time), I patted my coat pocket to see if my medication was in its usual place.

Good God, it wasn't there!

I nearly had another panic attack as I rushed back into my house to get the forgotten pills. When I found them and placed them into my coat pocket. I swear I could here a little voice say,

"Got you again."

It was at this time that I realized what had just happened. Even though I had not taken any of that medication for a long period of time, I was still mentally dependent on their physical presence in my coat pocket, **just in case.** I realized at that moment that I was still making concessions to this evil disorder, allowing it to keep its grip on me, thus dictating my behavior even though I didn't even know it until that moment.

When I made this **"Ah ha"** discovery, I threw the pills into the garbage along with the last remnants of this affliction. In so doing I regained my freedom and broke the chain that had bound me to the bad memories of the past. As long as I had continued to clutch my pocket each morning, I was feeding into my need for reassurance, even though I had no intention of ever taking another anti-anxiety pill. This **'just in case"** behavior is yet another weapon that the disorder has in its arsenal of tricks.

Don't buy it. Throw those pills away! If you can't, you still have work to do. Don't let this devil steal your freedom. You do not need the pills anyway. Why carry them and keep that chain to the past connected?

Make certain, if you were taking medications, you kick the habit under the supervision of the doctor that prescribed them in the first place.

Don't go "Cold Turkey."

5. THE BULLY SYNDROME

Agoraphobia is a bully that badgers and intimidates you into a fearful caricature of the person that you once were. It is a sad reality that this disorder is equipped with an astonishing arsenal of weapons that can be used to create fear and avoidance, thereby achieving its objective of domination.

Nearly everyone has had an encounter with a bully. Think about your own experience. Doesn't it sound like Agoraphobia is a bully? The only difference between the Agoraphobia bully and the others is, instead of a beating or some other form of torture, Agoraphobia chases you with the threat of symptoms. In either case, the act of running enables you to avoid the punishment, which is a reward for the bully, strengthening his control over you.

I am reminded of an experience that I had with a bully when I was about eight or nine years old. In this situation I was being bullied and tormented by a girl of about twelve.

She literally made my life a living hell. As the result I was constantly

Agoraphobia

modifying my behavior in order to avoid her.

I can still remember one spring afternoon running like hell toward home, with the bully hot on my heels. As I neared my house, I saw my father standing on the porch. At that moment, I had to make a decision. Should I continue running and let my father see me running from a girl or should I stand my ground?

Well, in this case it was an easy decision. I stopped; turned around and faced the bully ready to take whatever she had to offer. Her offer was a hard push which knocked me down.

When I got up, I was ready for action. I unloaded the biggest **"Haymaker"** known to mankind, which landed flush on her nose. Needless to say, her nose began to bleed, and that was the last time that she ever bothered me.

I had struck a blow for my own personal freedom. This act of courage accomplished two things. First, it enabled me to regain my self-respect and secondly, it taught me a valuable lesson which I would use years later while struggling with my own recovery.

When you face a bully, the bully will shrink and cease to be a threat. When you reward the action of the bully, he will grow stronger, while you grow weaker and more intimidated.

The exact same thing is true of the Agoraphobia bully. When you allow this bully to control your behavior by running and avoiding, you are reinforcing the domination that this bully has over you. When you face this bully, as I am encouraging you to do, it will shrink, and cease to be a factor in your life. The results are only as successful as you allow them to be.

6. THE TRUSTED COMPANION
This truism surprises many victims when they understand what is happening.

The surprise comes when they realize that they have endowed someone with the ability to keep the symptoms away. In other words you feel you can do things with your trusted companion that you are unable to do by yourself. Do you know why? You have once again accepted the fact that when you are with your trusted companion, you will not get the symptoms, therefore you can do just about anything.

Agoraphobia

Guess what? You are absolutely right. Unfortunately you have given all of the credit for this apparent miracle to your trusted companion, rather than recognizing the simple truth that it was your acceptance of the companion that made this so-called miracle happen. Example: Suppose you decide to go to a restaurant with your trusted companion, something you were unable to do by yourself. There you sit, feeling pretty good, and proud to boot. If only you could see and understand, at that time, what was really going on you could have told your trusted companion to leave because you didn't need his/her presence anymore.

What was really going on was your endowment of your companion with some kind of magical power that prevented the symptoms from coming, as you knew they would if you had attempted to do this by yourself. (**Acceptance**) The same thing is true of the disappearance of the symptoms when in the company of your trusted companion. (**Acceptance**)

Can you see the subtle trick you have used against yourself?

Don't misunderstand the value of your trusted companion, but give yourself some credit too. Once again you have accepted your companion as having the ability to diffuse the symptoms, while in actuality, it was you who created this ability. This truism applies in any situation that you enter with your companion. Can you see its applicability in your own situations?

Who is your trusted companion? Do you have one? Why do you trust him/her? More than likely you trust this person because you accept the fact that he will not judge you, or do any of the things that you think **(Accept)** everyone else will do, if you reveal your secret disorder. All of this stuff is going on without the knowledge of your trusted companion.

It is between you and the disorder. You have erected a foundation with your companion, upon which you can rely for strength and support, and your companion doesn't even know it.

Nice trickery! Bet you didn't know you were so clever.

As you can now see it is your acceptance of your companion's ability that is the key to this equation. And it is you who unlocks the equation and brings it to life. You need to become aware of this dynamic so that the credit goes to the appropriate per-

Agoraphobia

son. Remember the comment:

"**Most of us are unaware that we are unaware, becoming aware that we are unaware is a huge step.**"

7. THE SAFETY ZONE

The safety zone is a geographic area that you have accepted as being safe. It could be a neighborhood, a town, a store. The consistent theme, however, is acceptance. You have accepted the fact that you can do things within the safety zone that you cannot do outside of the safety zone.

You have erected a psychological barrier that enables you to avoid symptoms.

You can be safe within your zone, but not outside it, even though the same things are in each place.

You have accepted the fact that somehow things are different from one town to the next, or from one neighborhood to the next, when in reality they are the same.

"I will be safe here." **(Acceptance)**

Within the safety zone you can do anything you want to do, but outside that zone, it's a different story.

All of the activities that are possible within your safety zone are also

possible outside it, if you just Accept.

The barrier you constructed can only be removed by you. How do you remove it? You remove it by willingly doing the same things in one place that you do in the others. It makes no difference where you are, or what you are trying to do, the process is the same. **Acceptance.**

You are probably getting tired of seeing the word **Acceptance.** I realize that I use the word over and over. However, I will continue to use it because it is so critical to the entire recovery process. Please bear with me.

8. The Confidence Account

This is an account into which you can make either deposits or withdrawals, depending upon the situation.

In order to open the account, you have to borrow confidence from someone whom you trust (probably your trusted companion).

Once you have borrowed some confidence from this person, great things can begin to happen on your behalf. The confidence that you borrow will enable you to go into places and do things that previously you could not do. The beauty of this transaction is that there is no interest charge, and your trusted companion doesn't even know that he has loaned you some confidence. The mere fact that he is present is enough to complete the loan.

Can you see how this subtle transaction tilts the scales in your direction?

The use of this strategy will enable you to stop borrowing at some point and allow you to restore your own confidence level to the place where it rightfully should be. Once you have achieved this, you can become the person making the confidence loan. The major difference between you: the former borrower, and you: the confident lender, is the fact that you do not have to make the loan unknowingly, as your trusted companion did. You can teach someone who is trying to recover exactly what the trusted companion's role really is.

Nice little piece of knowledge.

9. BENEFITS OF AGORAPHOBIA

I can almost hear you asking, **"Is this guy nuts? What benefits are there in being an Agoraphobic? You must be** kidding. Doesn't everyone want constant panic attacks and scary symptoms? What do you mean, benefits of Agoraphobia?"

I can't blame you for being skeptical. After all, what possible benefits could possibly accrue from all of those horrible feelings? I am about to tell you. The most beneficial thing that results from having this disorder is the fact that you will never be caught by surprise. Do you know why? Take a guess.

In any situation or place in which you happen to be, you have already **"What if 'd . . .?"** every conceivable outcome and answered every **"What if . . .?"** question with a logical answer well in advance. Obviously this kind of pre-planning will absolutely guarantee that you will not be caught by surprise. Whether the **"What if . . .?"** has to do with a fire, a flood, car trouble, snowstorm, or sudden sickness, you will have already come up with a way to deal with the **"What if . . .?"** before it happens. It is a fact that a non-Phobic could be confronted by the same situation and not give either a second thought. As a matter of fact, they probably don't even know about the **"What if . . .?"** questions.

Agoraphobia

Ask yourself the following: Have you ever gone into a building, theater, etc., **and not checked out the exits?** I would be willing to bet you haven't. Most, including myself, will invariably do this so that we will know which exit to take in the event of an emergency.

One additional piece of information that I readily accept without reservation is that, even though I am completely recovered and have been for several years, I will always be an Agoraphobic. If this sounds like a contradiction, it really is not. The one major difference between me now and when I was at my worst, is the fact that I have taken the fear out of fear, it just doesn't matter. I am convinced that I still get the same symptoms that I got long ago, but since they don't matter, I don't know that I get them. You also will have the same experience as you reflect on your worst days and think about where you are now, and how far you have ome.

That is another benefit.

10. THE LAST FEAR BEFORE RECOVERY
As you get progressively better and begin to do more and more, there will

be one more obstacle to overcome.

It is not the same one for everyone. In my own case, it was being totally free to drive on the highway to any destination that I desired.

Yours may be different. Perhaps it is a fear-free trip to a mall, or dinner in a restaurant, a bicycle ride, a fishing excursion. Whatever the wish, it is the final fear that must be overcome before you can eliminate all the misery and become totally free.

Once you have decided that you will accept the challenge, you begin to feel edgy and strange. After wondering about these unusual feelings, it will dawn on you, as it did on me, that you are actually afraid that you have accepted this last challenge.

You are actually going to do something that previously terrorized you. How is that for a last ditch effort on the part of this demon to sidetrack you with the ultimate subtlety? Don't let it throw you. The fear that you are about to do the impossible is the last sneak attack that Agoraphobia will launch at you. You have taken the fear out of fear. Instead of **"What if...?"** and **"I can't . . ."** it will now be **"So what if . . . "** and **"I can... "**

Agoraphobia

This is the ultimate victory.

You have won and it will be a sweet victory. As each week turns into a month, and the months into a year, you might find yourself sitting in a traffic jam and begin reflecting back to that time when the mere thought of this situation would make you shiver with fear. Whether you realize it or not, that old demon is still trying to make the symptoms return, but to no avail. The symptoms just don't matter.

Your recovery is based upon an acceptance that the symptoms are of no medical significance, and, therefore, you allow yourself not to worry.

After all what is there to worry about? This final acceptance has destroyed the firing pin that once triggered all of those horrible, terrifying symptoms.

Congratulations! You have won. You made it!

I do not know how long it has been since you were able to function freely and lead a normal life. It really doesn't matter. What does matter is that you now have the ability to help yourself and also help someone else get off the Agoraphobia treadmill.

D. F. Nesto

CHAPTER 11

MYTHS THAT MISS THE MARK

There are two myths that I find particularly annoying. I have mentioned them in previous chapters:

"More Women Than Men Have Agoraphobia" in **Chapter 2** and **"Agoraphobia Causing Depression/Or Vice Versa "** in **Chapter 5.**

I am mentioning these two annoyances again because I continue to hear and read of these silly and ignorant statements being made over and over.

I know from personal experience that these statements are being made by people whose only knowledge of this disorder is through the study of it. There is certainly nothing wrong with researching and studying the disorder, as well as talking with its victims. I have a real problem with the fact that most, if not all, of the people making these statements are not, and never have been, Agoraphobic.

If they were, they would not make the statements. It is one thing to talk about this problem without experiencing any of its horrible feelings: panic, despair, hopelessness, isolation, and impending doom. It is quite another to know from experience just exactly what these feelings are all about. A victim is able to explain what he has experienced, but the explanation will only be meaningful to another victim. To anyone else, the explanation will fall on deaf ears that, at best, will only be able to create a feeling of sympathy on the part of the listener.

To paraphrase an old adage, "Let me not judge until I have walked a mile in his shoes".

Back to the myths.
"More women than men have Agoraphobia.

This myth is the most maddening of all. Not only is it untrue to a large extent, but it damages those of us who are men, by suggesting that we are less than masculine if we have Agoraphobia. This kind of garbage isolates us and creates an additional burden that has to be overcome. We have enough to deal with without some unthinking individual creating false burdens. First, we are forced to struggle with this horrible affliction that has rendered our lives a living hell and then, in addition, we are beset by a suggestions that we are dealing with a "woman's disorder."

How is a man supposed to avail himself of any hope of help when he is afraid and embarrassed to even admit that he needs it? It has been my experience that there are nearly as many men with Agoraphobia as there are women. The only real difference is that men do not report it, while women are more open about doing so. (I have known many women, however, who do not admit to the existence of this disorder, but for a variety of different reasons.) Can there be any wonder that men are afraid to admit to this disorder when given the mindless statements being made regarding gender?

Do not listen to them. I know from personal experience that the gender distribution of Agoraphobia is pretty even. I know this as the result of facilitating a number of support groups in which the men were not afraid to admit their affliction, because they were with people who "understood."

Having said all of this, I would like to suggest that this miserable myth be put to bed and never awakened again. As stated earlier, do not let this gender garbage deter you from following the suggestions outlined in these pages. Men and women alike must do the same things if they are to recover. There is no such thing as gender bias in the recovery process.

The other annoying myth is the notion that Depression Causes Agoraphobia.

"Agoraphobia causes depression"

Despite the claims to the contrary, it is my firm belief that, given all of the misery resulting from Agoraphobia, (i.e. isolation, destruction of self confidence and image, endless fear about everything, horrible, terrifying symptoms and last, but certainly not least, the total disappearance of a normal functioning human being), depression follows the onset of Agoraphobia. Now I ask you?

Who wouldn't get depressed? Depression causes Agoraphobia? I remain unconvinced.

Help Is But A Click Away -

A MESSAGE FROM THE PUBLISHER

In my troubled youth, I discovered the hope and knowledge available in self-help books. I subsequently became a psychologist and went on to write five self-help books. I was so impressed by the power of self-help books that when the Internet became so prevalent in our lives, I realized it was the ideal place for people to find help. *SelfHelpBooks.com* emerged and is readily available to anyone who is in need of help.

SelfHelpBooks.com publishes books by mental health professionals as well as by lay people who have coped with life's adversity and have valuable advice to pass on to the rest of us. The titles that can be found in *SelfHelpBooks.com*'s virtual bookstore have been carefully selected to provide help for a range of problems from addiction to depression, from fear to loneliness, and from problems of youth to problems of the elderly.

At *SelfHelpBooks.com* we think we have a book for almost every problem. If you need help immediately, you can download it as an E book. If you are in less of a hurry, you can order a print version and receive it within days.

If you visit SelfHelpBooks.com and don't find a book relating to your particular problem, contact us and we will immediately add books in that category. If you know of a particular self-help book that has helped you, let us know and we will add it to our list as well.

Harold H. Dawley, Jr., Ph.D., ABPP
Publisher

Printed in the United States
108421LV00001B/47/A